Lyons 'n Lions

By RL Lane

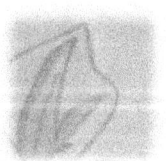

Illustrations by RL Lane

"Well, I am a lion. A Leo. Born on the 18th of August. But this book is not about me. It is about the bus. The Lyons Express..." RL Lane

It isn't just for the people of Lyons, NJ. There are only about 228 of them as of 2010. It is for the surrounding areas. It brings us daily to the Port Authority in the city. It starts out in my town. It waits in the dark for me to emerge from the trees and walk down the hill. The bus doesn't actually wait, but the driver inside does. He knows I'll eventually show up…

The whole operation is quite impressive. The Port Authority bus terminal is a major transit hub for many New Jerseyans. The terminal is the largest in the US and the busiest in the world by volume of traffic. It serves about 8,000 buses and 225,000 people on an average weekday…more than 65 million people in a year…

Many people sit inside those buses looking out the windows as they are transported back and forth. Some talk. Some sleep. Some think. Some read…

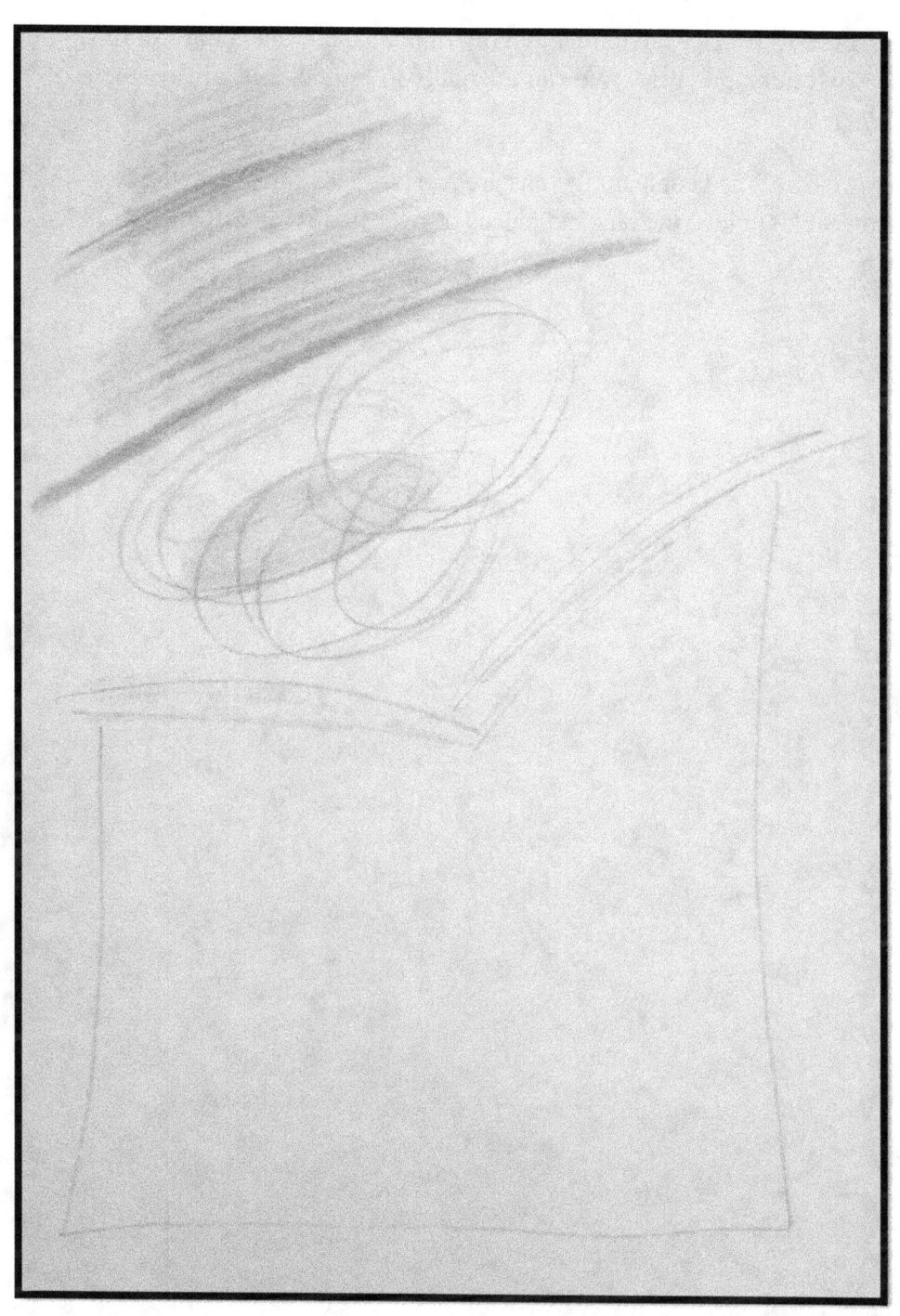

I draw. It helps me to feel that my time on the route is not lost time. I don't know why I think that way. We can't actually lose time. It is always there. Ticking away.

Many of the people on the bus are friends. Chatting about the day. I think the drivers like to hear the bits and pieces of lives that cross their way…

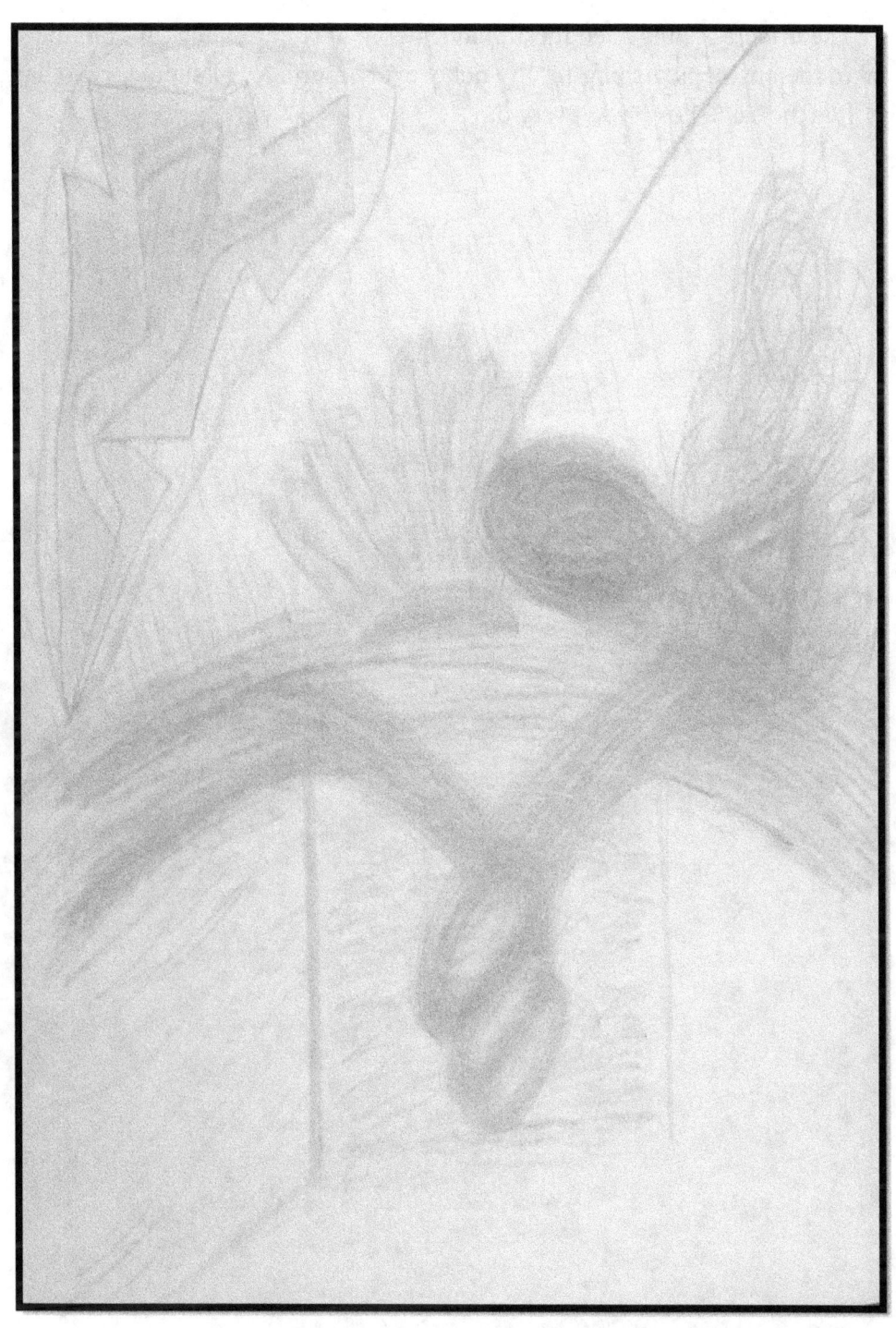

The drivers are the friendliest I have met in a while. I look up from the bottom of the bus steps, fishing for my ticket every morning. I should try to have it ready. It is the same bus I ride every day…

I went back to work in the city in the fall of 2015. I hadn't worked there since the 20's. My twenties. Not the 1920's.

Walking along the same streets that my once younger feet trod upon. Looking and seeing with a different set of eyes…

Every evening on my return trip there are men on the platform of the Port Authority directing people to get on the correct lines. The buses pull in and out, unload and load. The guy on the platform says I know where to go by now. He says I just stop to talk to him. It is true. You can't have a job like that without being a special kind of person. The stories he must have…

It reminded me of their history. This city does have a lot of history. I can see it. I can feel it in the terminal. I can see the ladies and gentlemen with their fine hats and fancy canes…

Before construction of the bus terminal, there were several terminals scattered throughout Manhattan. Some of them were inside hotels…

The All American Bus Depot on West 42nd…*all Americans, right this way!*

The Hotel Astor Bus Terminal on West 45th…*not an aster…that pretty purple flower, she wrote!*

The Dixie Bus Center on West 42nd, located on the ground floor of a hotel, opened in 1930 and operated until 1959...*oh Dixie...come on board!*

The Baltimore & Ohio Railroad had coach service aboard ferry to Communipaw Terminal in Jersey City. It was an elegant terminal with a revolving bus platform...*oh spin me 'round and 'round!*

Greyhound had its own facility adjacent to Pennsylvania Station and did not move into the bus terminal until 1963. By this time, all long-distance bus service to the city was consolidated at the terminal...

The Terminal Then

This way that way

Stop the bus!

This way that way

Move the bus!

This way that way

Wait for the bus!

This way that way

Get on the bus!

Ladies and Gentlemen!

The Terminal Now

That way this way

Hurry the bus!

Which way go away

Drive the bus!

That way this way

Wait for the ride!

My way your way

Pay the fair step right up!

Ladies and Gentlemen!

It is the holiday season. The buses are busier than ever. Everyone wants to get somewhere quicker. People should remember it's still the same distance between places as it was back in January. The bus needs the same amount of time to get from here to there. The December rush doesn't change that…

"I wanted to write this book so they could have a different look at the difference they make. How could I get to work in the city if the Lyons Express didn't have a stop in my small NJ town? The last stop on the end. Some days it is only me getting on or off at that stop. I do not have a car and the train commute is not as easy. I am thankful for the drivers and the directors who cross my path every day…" RL Lane

I hope in a small way this "thanks" makes them happy…

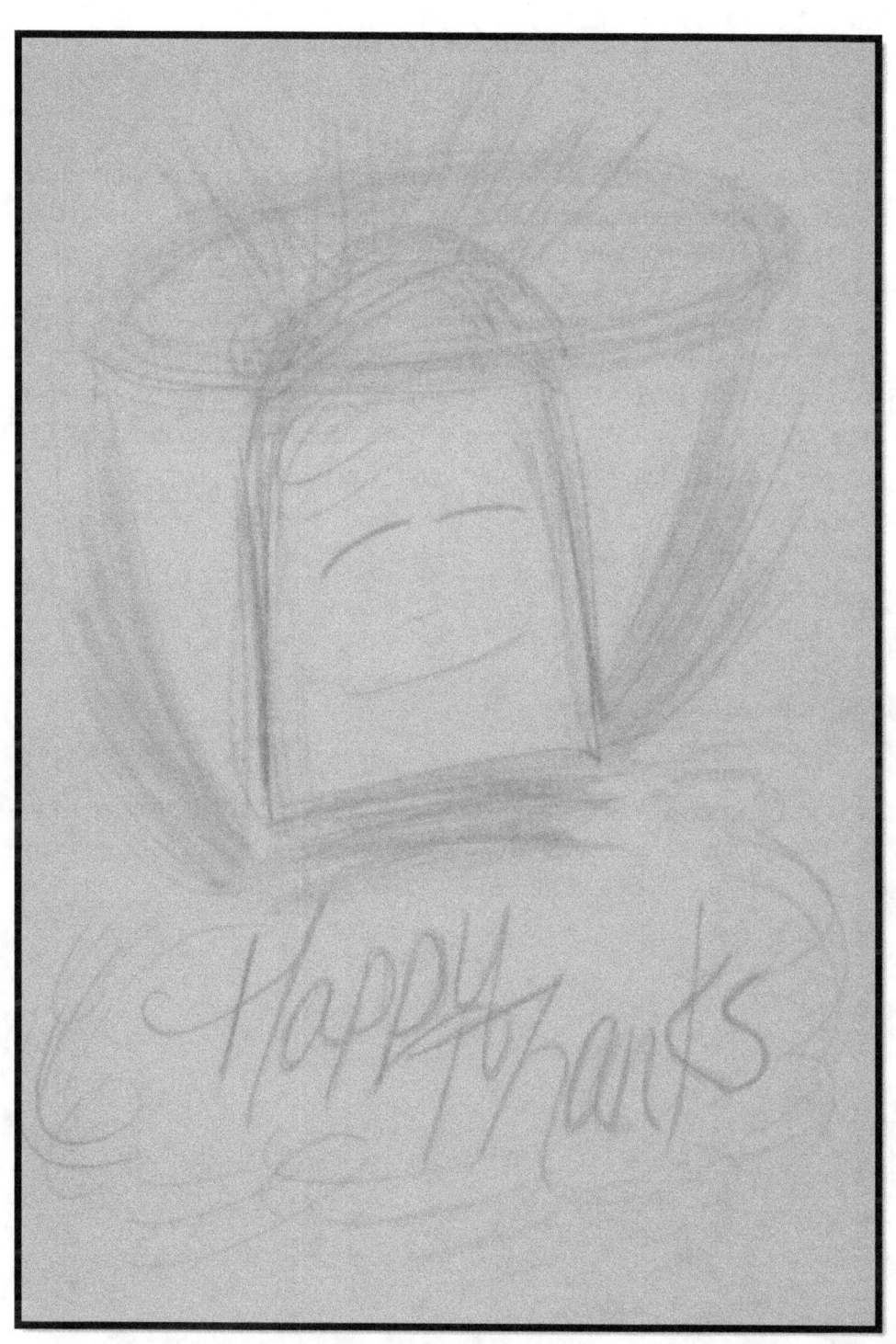

About the Author and Illustrator

RL Lane has published the EcarreT series and a collection of short stories featuring the illustrations, along with the children's books "G" and "How to Catch a Goast". The series begins with "Chapel Street Signs"…

…unexplained connections that challenge us to beli ve. A woman, a Dad a Doctor, a cat and mouse, a horse and tale tell their stories. "Do you beli ve in spirits?" I asked my friend. "Well look", he said, "I believe there are things that cannot be explained…" Oh. Plus, hear ov a Mom's battle with her struggle to connect to the woman...her little girl.

Welcome to EcarreT...a world
Where everyone cares
Why did I have to create it in...

A fiction fantasy world?

You may already know why, but you will see regardless of what you believe as a girl's journey of love and faith on her "Touring Machine" take her on the best journey of her mundane life. A life well on its way takes a turn in a direction that could've never been seen or even dreamed...

The author can be contacted at:

readrllane@gmail.com
www.Amazon.com/author/readrllane

Twitter.com/readrllane

Books by RL Lane

EcarreT Series:

Chapel Street Signs
secret Life OV an antE
Sri Town
Which of EcarreT

Hand of Heven

Bells to Believe

Short Stories:

Mon Treal, The Odd Cod, The Half Day, No Gift for Greed, Aunt Elm & Uncle Poc, What Would Caitlin Wear, The Bag of Scribbles, Mr. Uraly's Italy, A not G, Johnni and Georg, A Cup of Butter, The Walk of a THOUSAND Moods, Storm Window, The Rugs, Cones of Ice Crème, Angel-A, The Art of Sri Town, Under Water, The Dinner Party, The Vault, No Lines to Erase, Rock of Snow, Spilled Sugar, A Rug and a Bag, Polka Dot Rain Boots, The Stations

Children's:

G

How to Catch a Goast

A-Me

Coming Soon

Bubble ov lOVe

www.ingramcontent.com/pod-product-compliance
Lightning Source LLC
Chambersburg PA
CBHW081420170526
45166CB00010B/3417

* 9 7 8 1 5 2 2 8 0 5 8 9 2 *